I0616894

through the storm

through the storm

Michael Agnew

invite PRESS | Plano, Texas

through the storm

This book is printed on acid-free, elemental chlorine-free paper.

ISBN | 978-1-953495-45-7

22 23 24 25 26 27 28 29 30 31 —10 9 8 7 6 5 4 3 2 1
MANUFACTURED in the UNITED STATES of AMERICA

Dedication

This is for anyone who has felt like their voice didn't
matter. Your story holds power. The world needs to hear it.

To my wife Zara, thank you for always listening to these poems
when they were merely rambles in my journal. The steadiness
of your love is the anchor to all of this.

Table of Contents

Introduction to the Collection   6

Introductions   10
Make Art   12
Moments into Monuments   14
Family Ties   15
Rainbows   16
Masterpiece   17
Imago Dei   18
You Are More   19
Power of Your Words   20
Jumping off the Diving Board   22

Invisible Scars   24
Brighter Than Dark   25
Through the Storm   26
Lost in the Battle   27
God is Available   28
On the Edge   28
Lost for Words   30
Lost for Words II   31
Field Day   32
High Heels   33
Fatherhood   34
Toy Story Dad   35
Limbo Champion   36

Comparison   37
Pause   37
Fears   39
Under the Surface   40
Fly Away   42
The Riptide   43
People Pleaser   44
One Judge   45
Don't Be Normal   47

48   To Annie: A Breakup Poem
50   What is Love?
51   Uncrossed Lines
51   Speak Slowly
52   Empathy
53   Same God
54   What's Up with Pet Owners?
56   Time
58   Green Pastures
60   The Search for "IT"

62   Play-Doh Jesus
64   Complacency
65   Doing vs Being
66   Clean as Dirt
66   Good Intentions
67   Fully Connected / Immensely Lonely
68   Confessions of a Technology Addict
70   Loneliness of Social Media
71   Copycat Creations
72   Does Anyone Know That You're a Christian?
73   Secret Faith
74   As One
76   Before the Red Sea

77   Except Me / Accept Me
78   Content with the Fine Print
79   Bruised Cheeks
80   Death by Suicide
81   Trick or Treat
82   End the Stigma
83   Simple Days
84   Repentance I
86   Repentance II
88   Repentance III

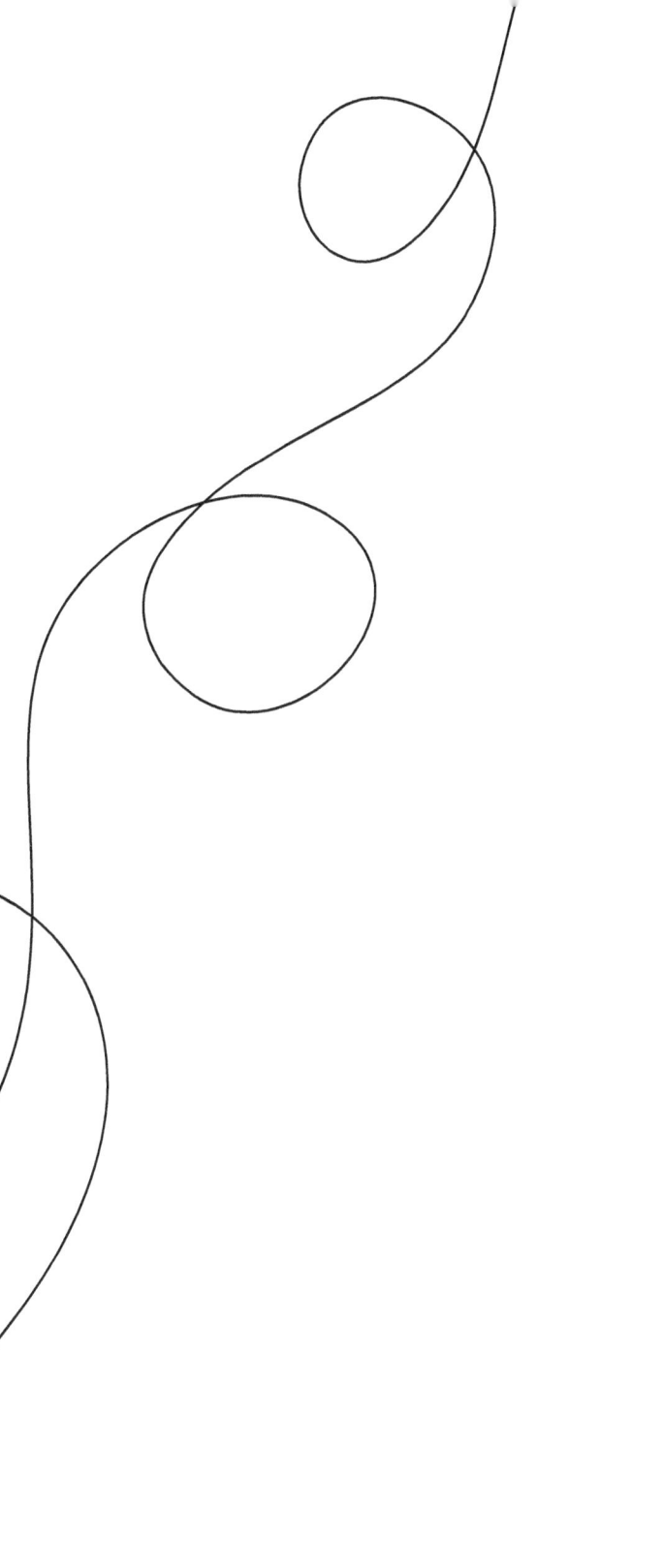

Introduction to the Collection

I have found no better way to express my thoughts and feelings than through poetry.

I grew up with a noticeable stutter. Often, the words in my head have landed more easily on paper than in someone's ears. As a result, I developed a love for writing, not the kind of writing that yielded short stories or essays, but the beauty and intimacy of poetry. My poetry comes from a primal place, a place in which what I think and feel, how I experience the world, myself, and God, streams forth onto the page as a kind of visual art, a group of emotional sculptures made of words.

The depth and emotion that a poem can deliver is unlike any other form of communication. No individual poem is the same. If you gave a poetry writing prompt to a group of ten people, everyone's poem would be different. Some would rhyme. Some would use minimal words to convey deep meaning. Some would use words in excess to overembellish a point. Some would be structured with lines and stanzas, while others would freely flow with no method. Each poem would be unique because each writer is unique. Poetry at its core is the expression of the emotions and feelings of its creator.

Poetry has shaped my life and has given me an outlet in which to use my stutter-filled voice in a way that I never would have thought possible and to express the emotions inside of me in a way unique to my life and experience. Yet, I believe that as human beings, we resonate with each other's feelings, with our joys and our tragedies. I hope that this book of my outpourings will resonate with you and that you too will experience the joys and sorrows of humanness that we all share through the poems in this volume.

Recently I stumbled upon the *Passion Translation* of one of my favorite verses, Ephesians 2:10, and this favorite verse of mine took a completely new meaning. The TPT says: "We have become his poetry, a re-created people that [sic] will fulfill the destiny he has given each of us, for we are joined to Jesus, the Anointed One."

Yes, you read that right. This verse says we are God's poetry. I am God's poem. You are God's poem. I am a poem who makes poetry. Now before any theological scholars start trying to poke holes in this life changing new layer to my favorite verse, here's where that translation originated.

The Greek word in Ephesians 2:10 indicating "poetry" is *poiema*. It means "something made." But it is from this word *poiema* that the English words poetry and poem were derived. I believe that if we allow this beautiful truth to take root in our hearts, then it has the potential to change our lives and the lives of those we connect with daily. I believe that poetry can change the world, and I believe that together we can change the world. Because whenever we take the emotions and the feelings that are inside of us and express them by creating poetry, it allows others who have experienced similar emotional journeys to connect with these experiences in powerful ways. That is why hearing a poem or a song about a broken heart draws people in. They have experienced that same feeling before. They connect with the poetic expression of that feeling on a deeply personal level, but also on a communal level. They know that they are not alone in these feelings.

I believe that there is no greater desire for a human being than to be known and feel like your experience is something shared with others. We want to know that we are not alone and that others have been through similar emotional journeys as we have. That is why people can look at a painting and see themselves in the artwork, even though it's not their work. It's not their hands that created it, but they see themselves in that story. It allows them to resonate with the artist.

I believe that we have to know the power that art (and poetry) has in people's lives in order for us to fully know the power of Ephesians 2:10. We are God's artistic expression. Everything we have ever been a part of, every failed relationship, every accomplishment, every embarrassing story, every night crying ourselves to sleep, every burned bridge, every milestone celebration: God wants to use those moments to show others that they are not alone. God wants to use the stories of our victories and our failures, so that people can know that it is through God's grace that they are saved.

Sometimes we feel, we are defined only by our victories. But God works through our failures just as much as our victories. Perhaps more. Our failure stories are also our redemption stories. When we share our redemption stories, it assures others that there is always hope.

In the following pages I have shared some of the poems that I have written over the years, many of which have lived their lives in journals and have never been seen by another soul. But if I am to live out the truth of Ephesians 2:10, that God created me as His divine poetry, then I need to express my victories and failures to the world, so that others might connect with them and recognize God's grace in their own lives from within these lines.

If God can radically redeem a timid, stuttering boy and see in him a masterpiece, then God can do the same for you as well. May this collection touch your heart, as it has compelled mine.

Michael Agnew
August 2022

Introductions

I am from a suburb of Houston
but swangaz and screwtapes were more legend
than reality in my world

I am from a town called Pearland
but don't let the name trick you
my eyes hadn't seen a pear tree until I got to college

A college that was paid for by my hardworking grandparents
who sold their business of 30 years
so their grandkids could get the education
that they never had

I am from a home that subscribed
to the culinary arts of Marie Callender's frozen meals
because my mom was often sick
and my dad often worked nights
frozen chicken fried steak on TV trays
is what held my family dinners together most nights
you can't microwave familial bonds
but you can microwave the food that keeps it together

I am from a family that oozed love to the moon and back
with parents who told me daily how proud they were of me
so when my stutter often made me feel friendless at school
my home was the place that I daydreamed of
being back with my two younger brothers
each of us two years apart
I hardly have a memory they aren't in
I will stand by their side until the end

I am from a church home that urged its members
to invest into the youth
they saw my purpose way before I did
they watered and nurtured that purpose in me
faster than the heat rays of the school bullies
could wilt it away

I wouldn't be here if it weren't for them
the ones who put me on stages when fear held me in cages
the ones who showed up again and again and again
the ones who painted the picture of God's relentless pursuit
of me through their pursuit of me

My life is the testimony
of how a loving home and a loving church
can overpower the coldness of the world

Make Art

As created creatures whenever we create art
we reflect something innate in who we are
Like how God painted the skies with the stars
We create beauty when we put on display what is ours

through eighth notes and brushstrokes
through harmonies and melodies
through metaphors and vocal chords
through poetry and photography

All of these contain one common thread
An artist using their tools to create an extension
of them
Which extends past space and time
As their artistic expression ruminates in our minds
That's why I can hear Bach's composition for the 20th time
And still feel his heart intertwine with mine
Because when you create something that had no form
and give it meaning
When you see what could be and shape it into being
You create possibilities and dreams
And hopes that life is more than it seems
You create change
Small shifts that cause the world to re-frame
You create an empowering confidence
That every voice matters and everyone is an artist
You create joy and tangible happiness
In the depression of life, art brings beauty to the darkness

We were all a blank canvas that became a masterpiece

Each of us crafted with purpose and thought
And now the masterpiece becomes an artist
Created to make art that reflects our God

For God is beauty
And when we make beautiful things, He is praised
So make art
Make beautiful things
Share that special spark that is inside of you
Because when you do, the world is changed

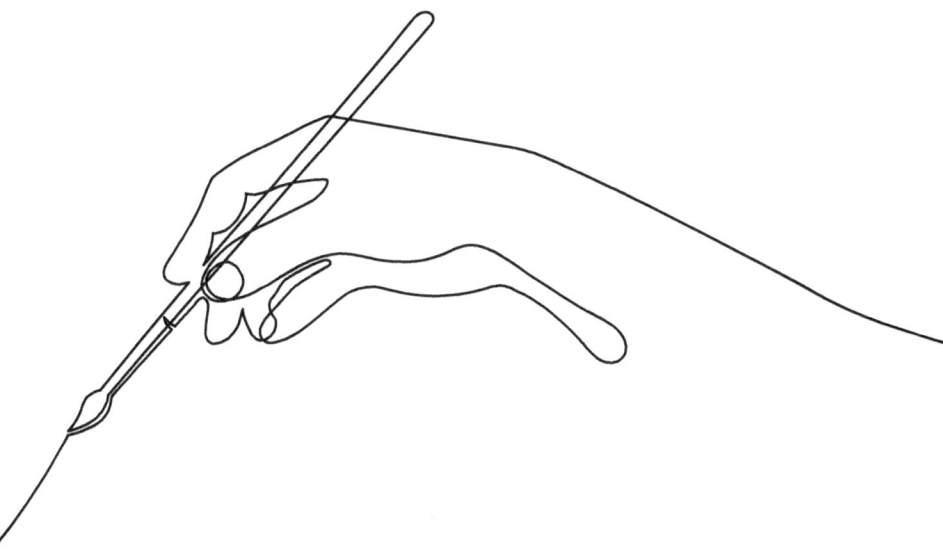

Moments into Monuments

I've been told I'm quite the storyteller
I make the mundane seem extraordinary
I can make any average grocery store run
seem like the final suitcase in Deal or No Deal
and I just won a million dollars
all because I grabbed the last bag of Starburst Jellybeans
and I felt like a hero returning from war

I can turn any moment into a monument
make the mediocre feel so monumental
by just adding N and U
a couple of letters and
you can construct statues to immortalize the life
that was lived and the stories within

Why settle for boring?
Why wait for something to change when you can be the change?
All it takes is to switch your perspective
Adventure is out there
You just have to build it

Family Ties

you have worth because of who made you
no mistake could ever take that away
the Father's heart has infinite love for you
all of your debt has already been paid

before you were born your future was purchased
your past has been covered so regret no more
the God of the universe made you with intention
where you are in the present was thoughtfully prepared

what you have done does not remove your title
a Child of God you will be forevermore
your hands might be muddy
and your heart might be bruised
but that crown on your head cannot be removed

Rainbows

you were created by the creative Creator
the base of all beauty and art
who brought life from the dark
with only goodness in God's heart

beginning with speaking existence into galaxies
weaving words like tapestries
to forming humans from dust
God sculpted and molded each one of us

with the world as a blank canvas
God made it beautiful
alive and musical
flowing and fruitful
intricately wonderful

from the trillions of stars that speckle our skies
to the special sparkle in our eyes
when we see a rainbow for the first time

a rainbow

full of every living color
a creative covenant like no other
covering us with the promise
that was prophesied by the prophets
and fulfilled by Christ's providence

we were created to be creative
and use our free will
to be innovative in our worship
so with beauty like a rainbow
live youraife as the reflection
of the creative Creator

Masterpiece

you are so beautiful
the most wonderful treasure in God's eye

you are purposeful
because God took intentional time
crafting every inch of your design

you are perfect

you are not a mistake
or to be seen as second rate

you are a masterpiece

with every quirk and every trait
crafted exactly as you were meant to be made

you are worth more than you can ever imagine

you are the last thing from average

you are set apart

from the very start
when there was no light or dark
you were already a part of God's glorious plan

because you are a masterpiece

Imago Dei

on your best day or your worst day
your identity does not change
you are made in the image of God
and that image cannot be erased

the debt that was paid is permanent
your position has been sealed in place
your sins have been forgiven
so do not live another moment in shame

you are the clay in the Potter's hands
God has crafted your every piece
a masterpiece is your identity
because that is what the Master speaks
so the next time you look in the mirror
see what the Master sees

God's child
the Imago Dei
the Holy's Spirit's temple
a saint
through God you are one
and that will never change

You are More

You are more than a relationship.
You are more than your education.
You are more than what you see in the mirror.
You are more than your insecurities and fears.

You are more than the opinion of a guy.
You are more than what clothes you buy.
You are more than a college acceptance letter.
You are more than a grade from a professor.

You are more than a label.
You are more than an athlete.
You are more than the quiet guy.
You are more than a band geek.

You are strong.
You are victorious.
You hold power.
You are a warrior.
You are special.
You are unique.

Regardless of whatever label the world tries to put on you
You are exactly who God made you to be.

Power of Your Words

W O R D S.

The most powerful instrument that you possess.
They can give life or they can bring death.
They can lift high or they can oppress.
They can fall deaf or they can take breath.
But nonetheless, one simply cannot forget the power
of what those words meant.

W O R D S.

They scar.
They leave hidden little marks.
little remarks that seem so innocent but truly aren't.
Passive aggressive barbs that pierce into your flesh
like glass shards.
They have no regards for their victims.
Sin is the problem, but words are the symptom.

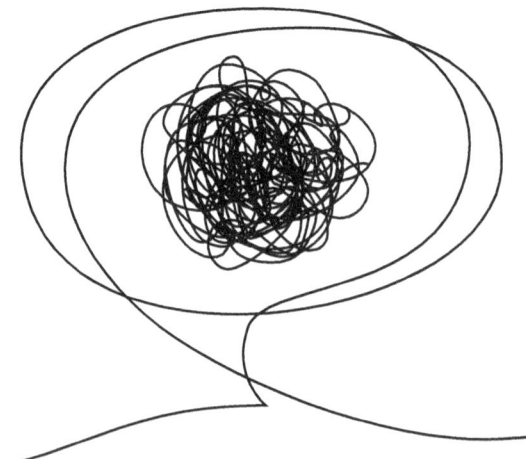

W O R D S.

Projectile utterings shooting faster than a gun.
There's no going back once they leave your tongue.
I'm rubber and you're glue.
What you say to me bounces back and sticks to you.
If only these words were actually true.
But elementary school rules don't exist in the real world.

There're no take backs
no mishaps
no zig zags
or this that
your syntax is in tact

and rips back like whiplash

W O R D S.

What can take a second to say can live
in someone's bones for a lifetime.
Off the cuff remarks can cut deeper
than you realized.
And hold more weight than you desired.
Getting the final word in is never required.
Because your tongue is a knife.
It can bring life or it can cut through and slice
Past all of the nice compliments and likes
to expose our deepest fears and frights.

Jumping Off the Diving Board

Why is it that I can remember how Brittany Johnson
made fun of my s s s t u t t e r
on my first day of sixth grade
better than I can remember my own wedding day?

Or how even to this day
I can hear the e c h o of the l a u g h t e r
from my eighth grade English class
every time that I was asked to read something out loud?

Or how every time that I shake a stranger's hand
and my tongue strangles out the words
"h h hello m my
name is m m michael."

My throat tenses up
my mind begins to race
and even though I know the words to s s say
they stand on the t t tip of my tongue
like a child frozen on a diving board
too afraid to j j jump off

As I push those words out of my closed throat
every syllable has bounced
b a c k and f o r t h
a dozen times in my mind
before they finally decide to leave my mouth

I have more unspoken words than you will ever speak
in your lifetime

My stutter is like
the torn ACL of a fifty five year old ex-high school
football phenom
except that my speech impediment
isn't an injury of my past
as I reminisce on memories that I will never get back
my stutter is **fully alive**
and loves to still announce itself
in the most inconvenient m m m oments

That is why my greeting to you isn't casual
it has been tirelessly **rehearsed**
in bedroom mirrors throughout my adolescent years
every time that I introduce myself to someone new
I c c crawl through a battlefield
of old scars and tears
of conquered **fears**
To deliver to you a story of redemption
What you hear as a record s s s kipping
I hear as p p p erfection

> That is why instead of **silencing** my voice
> for fear of my stutter being exposed
> I hold my words **center stage**
> unafraid to reveal them

So no, I'm not trying to pause for dramatic effect
my brain is just trying to encourage my tongue
to trust itself
because the water is safe.
The best entrances are those that make the biggest **splash**
so my stutter will c c cannonball
through the deepest waters
and show everyone that I choose to be **brave.**

Invisible Scars

my scars are something that you cannot see
but i still feel them
while my initial wounds have scarred over
their lasting mark remains
they now stand as a picture of triumph through pain

these scars are now me
and i won't hide them in shame
i will hold them up high
as a symbol of change
what was old is made new
put my scars on display
i've been given new purpose
i won't dwell in self-hate

these scars are the proof
that God can heal the deepest wounds
they serve as reminders of the painful struggles
that i have been through
and the new life in its place
that continues to bloom

what was weakness now strengthens
i'm a product of grace
my scars tell the story
of a Voice led by faith

Brighter Than Dark

Light is brightest when it's in the darkest places
With God inside us there is nothing that can take us
Even in the fiercest storms as our growing fear enrages
Nothing in the slightest is stronger
than the God of our Salvation

God is in the wind and in the silence
God has seen what's been and what's behind us
God knows what is with all future knowledge
So trust and believe
That God is your Provider

Through the Storm

in times of troubles i put my worries
on the creator of all the created
when my present seems like it's about to vanish
i remember that God is the one who made it
and all my worrying won't save it

when a ship is out at sea
and the water is fully raging
sailors don't try to tame it
they ride out the waves
knowing that if they push through
then they are going to make it

they know what is in their control and what isn't
their spirit might bend but will not break
they are resilient
when the fear comes
they acknowledge their feelings
and then stand to face their fear
until the storm is finished

because the thing about storms
is there's a calm that precedes it
and it always returns like before

the winds might whip you back and forth
and death seems to move towards you
but as long as you hold your course
the calm is coming and peace will be restored

Lost in the Battle

i'm so quick to discredit
like the past has been shredded
forgetting all the times that your love has been present
my goals feel threatened
and my ego's invested
so my mind is telling me things that don't fit
with your message
i know you're omnipresent
i know that you're transcendent
i know these things
i know these things
but i'm feeling so lightheaded
like where's my life headed?
i'm lost with no direction
as i'm walking bare chested
in the battle unprotected
as my cries are being deafened
on their way up to heaven

God is Available

When life is full of **problems**
and you don't know how to solve them
and the **storm** isn't calming

Remember that God is **available**.

When God feels out of touch
and life is just **too much**
and you can't take one more punch

Remember that God is **available**.

When life is beyond busy
and you don't have a minute
and your head just keeps on **spinning**

Remember that God is **available**.

When you get **rejected**
and the outcome is unexpected
and you don't know what your next step is

Remember that God is **available**.

When your love has lost the spark
and your marriage is in the **dark**
and there's only bitterness in your heart

Remember that God is **available**.

When your voice isn't heard
and you start to **question** your worth
and you just want to end the hurt

Remember that God is **available**.

On The Edge

Sometimes life feels too much
Sometimes God seems out of touch
Sometimes it feels like you're being crushed
And giving up seems like the only the option

But the thing is
Whenever you reach that point
When you are so close to the edge
and you're holding life together with a thread
and it feels like there's no light ahead
God steps in
and says:

I am with you
My hand is over you
I am going to come through for you
just trust in what I do

trust Me
lean into Me
enjoy My presence
and let Me make you into something
that you could never imagine

Lost For Words

God I love you
and right now I need you
My faith is weak
Holy Spirit please breathe through
all my weaknesses and doubts
so I can be near you
Because this storm is too much
for me to even see through
Because like that night
You aren't there.

I don't know why tragedy comes
and why you don't always intervene
Wouldn't a God of miracles
have stopped their car from hitting that tree?

Why is it that you're absent?
Why is it that you're distant?
You could've saved them in an instant
So did you miss it?
Did you listen?
Did you hear their cries?
God, do you hear mine?

I'm told you're always there but I need it to be true!
I trust you Lord
You know that I do
but I can't help but ask…
where in this broken world are you?
Because this wasn't supposed to happen
I can't believe that it was
It's times like these I see you more like a Judge

This is beyond just not fair
Lord did you just not care?
I'm at a loss for words
and I think I'll just stop there.
Because like that night
You aren't there.

Lost For Words II

My child, I'm here
I know that you cannot see this situation clear
but I was so near
I was with them through every tear
Please know that my heart is broken like yours
What happened is not what I had in store
My plan does not include war
but sometimes a battle happens that I am not for

I did not create the tragedy
But I was there when it happened
They did not die alone
I had angels by the thousand
Who comforted them in their pain
and escorted them up the mountain

I wish that it wasn't this way
I wish that you didn't feel pain
I wish that you could see the sun through the rain
But one day you will
and when you call My name
I will be there in an instant
and you will fully see My face

I cannot wait to hold you
and tell you that I am so proud
I know your screams are loud
and I hear every sound

Please know that this is not the end
and earth is not your home
I might feel distant in this moment
but your pain is always known
I promise that one day all the mysteries will be shown
But until that day rest assured
that you are never alone

Field Day

i remember the first time that i realized my best
wasn't good enough
it was field day
third grade
and we had to race in a thirty yard dash
out of thirty people
i came in third to last
as i crossed the finish line
all of my friends just laughed

    and every now and then when i look in the mirror
    all of those memories flood back

to their laughs
their sighs
their haphazard nice tries
the compliments that are really white lies
i can see the truth in their eyes
i know what they see

    someone who will never be good enough.

High Heels

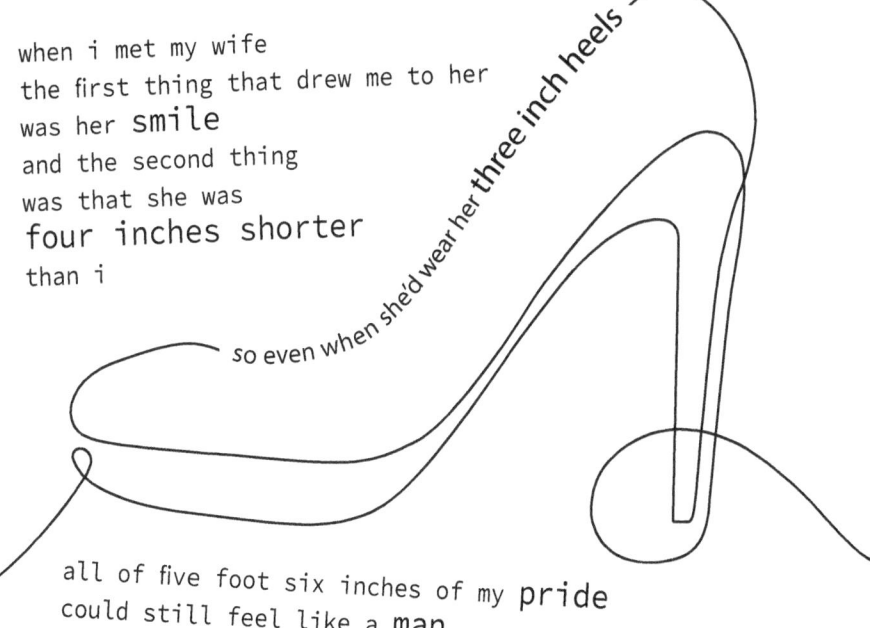

when i met my wife
the first thing that drew me to her
was her smile
and the second thing
was that she was
four inches shorter
than i

so even when she'd wear her three inch heels

all of five foot six inches of my pride
could still feel like a man

Fatherhood

There's no greater feeling
than walking through the door
after a hard day's work
and hearing the words
"daddy I missed you"

Arms wrapped around my leg
Your face buried in my thigh
As I pick you up with your arms stretched high

Suddenly you're SUPERMAN

Flying in the sky
And all the stresses of the workday
Fall down to the side
Faster than a speeding bullet

Nothing surprised me more than
When I first held you

Your body felt like air
But I could hardly move my arms
Because I was paralyzed by the reality that
Your lips looked just like mine

Fatherhood felt so light and so heavy at the same time

Toy Story Dad

I used to watch *Toy Story* and think of my toys
But now I watch *Toy Story* and think of my boys
And wonder about the things that they're going to enjoy
And wonder about the things that I want them to avoid

Like when life stretches you too thin
like you're Slinky Dog
And all of your plans come crashing down
like so many Lincoln Logs
Living like an Alien trying to reach the Claw
Only to reach the top where you see how far you've gone
Thinking that you're flying
but you're just falling with style
Like Mr. Potato Head life's in pieces in a pile
About to go Hamm but you're off by miles
Living like Sid but there's sadness behind the smile

The world has a lot more Lotsos than Woodys
But love is a lasso that will pull you
back to me
Yes school playgrounds can be packed
full of bullies
But the name on the bottom of your shoe
loves you fully

Don't just focus so much on the Bullseye
that you fall off the horse
Life can get rocky
but just follow the course
The days might feel slow
but time moves in Light Years
You always Got a Friend in Me
I promise I'll be right here

Limbo Champion

sometimes i wonder what it would feel like
to look in a mirror
and not instantly see all of my shortcomings
or what it would feel like
to walk into a room and actually feel like i belong there

that's why i'm so good at laying low
in the background

but eventually you can put yourself down so much
that the ground gets more comfortable
than using your legs
so you slide on your belly like a serpent
slithering its way underneath the lowest bar
of expectations

i have become the best person i know at limbo

at least i finally found something that i'm good at

Comparison

comparison
compare the sin
come pair the sin
against any of mine
and they will fit perfectly on that dotted line
where Jesus Christ has signed

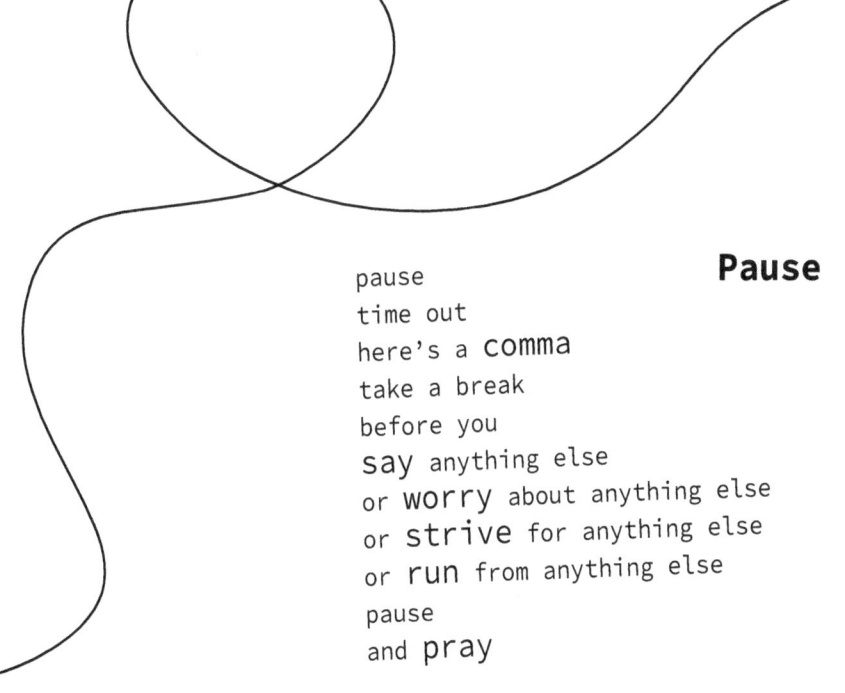

Pause

pause
time out
here's a comma
take a break
before you
say anything else
or worry about anything else
or strive for anything else
or run from anything else
pause
and pray

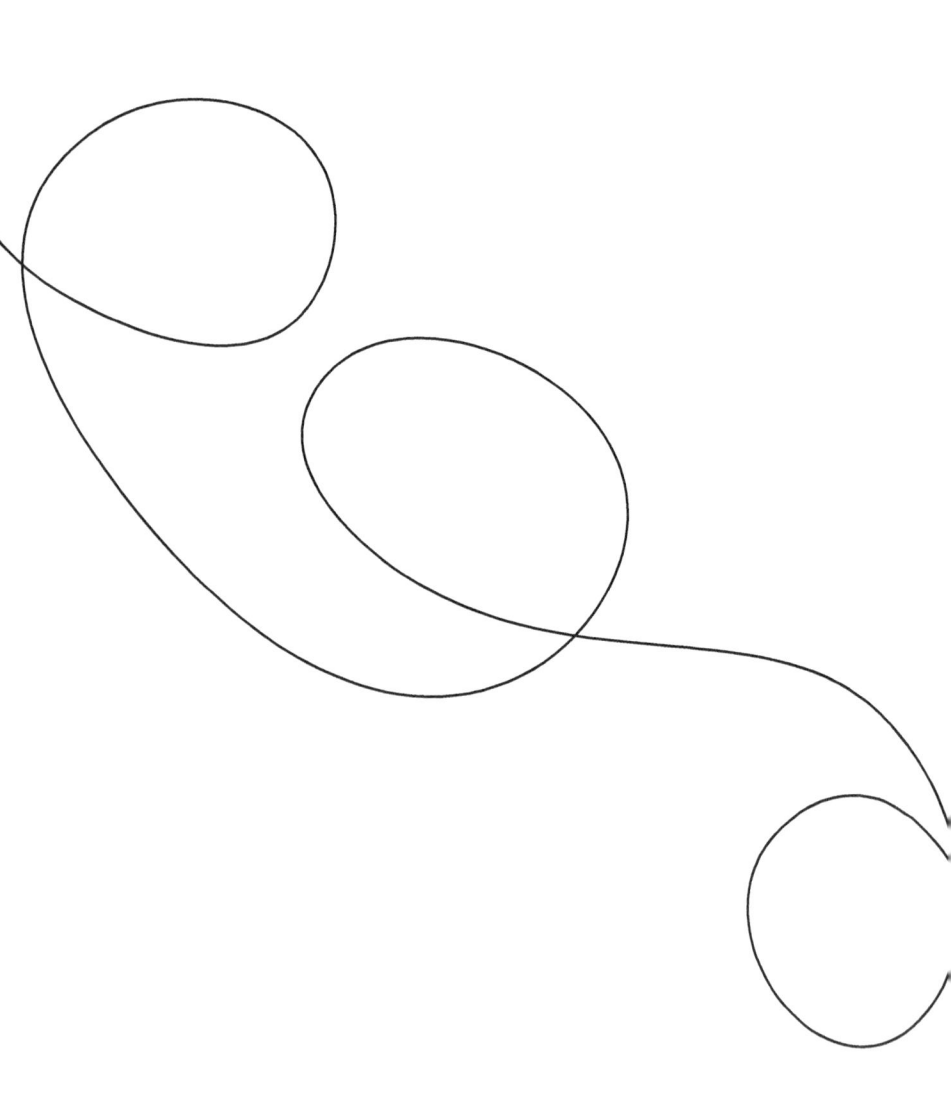

Fears

I'm afraid of a lot of things:
i'm afraid of the dark
of public speaking
of dying alone
of those awkward greetings
(where they go for a handshake
and i go for a knuckle bump
and i end up looking like an absolute chump)
i'm afraid of looking dumb
(i mean there's so much to overcome)
i'm afraid of being mugged
i'm afraid that i didn't actually find true love
i'm afraid that my wife will wake up one morning
and say she's had enough
and that i'll end up like one of those guys
on the street corner
just asking for some spare quarters

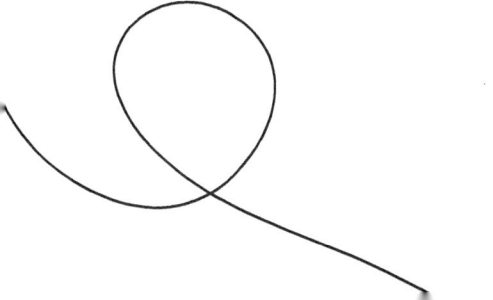

Under the Surface

no matter how old i get
i can't seem to loosen the grip
of fear from my lips

i used to have a stutter and a lisp
and for years my s's would "thound like thith"

and that embarrassment runs so deep
to where even now the brief remnants of my stutter and lisp
play a much bigger emphasis on my life than i care to admit

under the surface my mind can't seem to forget
the not too silent diss from the kids
in middle school saying
"silly Michael spit it out"
"he sounds like porky the pig with a sponge in his mouth!"

soaking up all of the S syllables with my tongue
as I stumbled over my words
until i just stopped speaking
so my stutter wouldn't be heard
i know that may sound absurd
but i used to think i was just this little dude
whose throat swelled up in interviews
for fear that stuttering is not what winners do

But miraculously one day God said
"Michael, in your weakness my glory will shine through."

I don't fully know what happened
It was definitely not from any of my actions
But like a Holy Spirit chemical reaction
My fear of my stutter was overcome

So now my life is dedicated to those who think
they don't have much to offer
Who think that God can't use them because
they are too awkward
My poetry is for the ones who think no one notices
Whose days are filled with hopelessness

I am living proof that YOU have a purpose
And that your testimony is so much deeper
and so much more thaust what is on the surface

Fly Away

Sometimes I want to fly away

like a bird

And forget some of the things that I've heard
I can't believe the nerve of these words
Where did they learn to bring so much hurt?

The Riptide

anxiety brings so many emotions
and i don't know why i feel them
it's like i'm caught

in the riptide of the ocean

and i can't be reeled in
so i smile over my insecurities
trying to conceal them
but putting bandaids over wounds
never really heals them

People Pleaser

i've always been a people pleaser
a pushing past what's painful pleaser
a laughing at unfunny jokes pleaser
a playfully bypassing problems pleaser

i'm paralyzed whenever it comes to telling people
my opinions
i've fought so hard to not look or seem different
at my core i crave acceptance
and it's so much easier to just fit in

so i hold my lips shut until my face turns blue
just so i don't have to tell you what i really think of you
i would rather withhold until i have no breath left
in my lungs
because i like being liked
more than i like telling you that you're wrong

so i will swallow my tongue
look over any bad blood
over-emphasize peace and love
all the while being unaware of the damage
that my closed lips have done

i will please people no matter what it takes
i just like to keep things safe
i mean caring for the needs of others
is a wonderful character trait
that is until you carry so many unspoken things
that your character breaks

One Judge

a lot of people in this world will tell you how to live
but their talk is thin
they pocket sins
the tongue they mock you with
is rooted in what made the Fall begin

pride

you're insecure in where your value is
so you bring others down
to make yourself feel big
but there's only one person who's death erased your sins
and judgment is only His to give

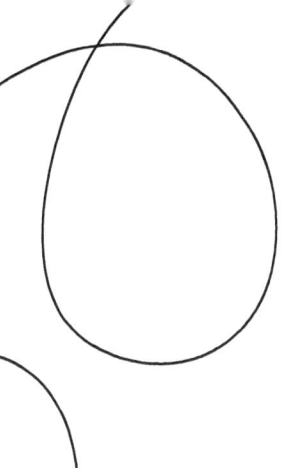

Don't Be Normal

there is no one who can break you
no one who can take you
no one who can shake you
because the one who created you
is bigger than all of that

God is bigger than all of your fears
bigger than all of those tears
from all of those years
of crying out just wanting to be normal
but He doesn't use those who are normal
God uses those who are willing
willing to be themselves

so be you
the individual
the uniquely created
special and sacred
individual

You

your scars, share them
your broken hearts, wear them
don't let them tear down who you are
to where you become someone that you aren't
don't let your pursuit of normal
cover up what makes you, you

be willing to be you
because when you do
God's poetry shines through
And causes others to do the same too

To Annie: A Breakup Poem

i'm in an unhealthy dating relationship with anxiety
we've been on again and off again
more times than a Kardashian
but no matter the victories
she always pulls me back in

she has me wrapped around her finger like a piece of candy
always telling me what i can't be
she gets in the way of my friends and family
i try to reason with her
but she's not very understanding

with your ordinary pair of eyes
you might not see the hurricane that she brings
to my paradise
but when she steps in the room I become paralyzed
acutely aware of the paradigm

i just can't do small talk
i feel like my awkwardness is nonstop
insecurities begin ringing in my head
like an alarm clock
and as soon as i step down this hole
anxiety's power on me has become unlocked

she reminds me of how my addiction to coffee
has discolored my teeth
and how sometimes i only close one eye whenever i blink
paranoid to not give an unintentional wink
to a stranger that might interpret it
as a romantic nonverbal cue that i did not mean
and now i have a million negative thoughts
racing inside of my head
insomnia hits as i lay in my bed
because now i can't stop thinking about
what my high school ex said
when she dumped me because she wanted
to date my best friend instead

those memories echo around in my cave of self-doubt
and everyone wonders why i'm always spaced out
because annie has me wound up so tight
and i can't let myself down
it's like i'm trapped in her web of lies
and i see no way out

so anxiety this is our breakup poem
because this relationship that we have cannot keep going
it's time to let you go and stop letting you control me
but if i'm not real with myself then you can't be beat
so today i refuse to remain a slave to anxiety
annie, you no longer have control of me
goodbye anxiety

What Is Love?

what is love?

        is it a feeling?
        is it a verb?
        is it something that is seen or heard?
        is it more than a word?

    can love be bought?
    can it be replicated?
    because love has so many cliché statements
    that have gotten copy and pasted
    love has lost sight of where its home base is

you see love is a feeling, but it's also a mindset
love can cause sickness and blindness
it can be said but never felt
love can be so hot it causes a heart to melt
or be so cold that you feel its stings every time
that you're not held

                love does not fit neatly in a box
                love cannot be bought
                but it does come at a cost
                and it requires a lot
                a lot
                a lot
                of self-less thought

one day love will go from needing cootie shots
with circle, circle, dot, dots
to being much more messy than not

    and just when you clean it up
    it spills out again
    because love's work is never done
    but love is worth the mess

Uncrossed Lines

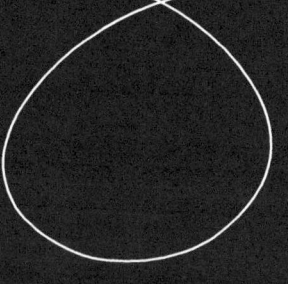

Pause =
a brief moment of silence to collect your thoughts
before your tongue reaches a line
that might not need to be crossed

Speak Slowly

slow down and ask yourself:
does there need to be an answer?
can you just listen without offering an opinion?
don't be so quick to speak
that you keep healing from coming to the surface
maybe your presence is all that is needed in that moment

Empathy

what would happen if we decided to put our judgments
on pause?
instead of needing to perform instant surgery
on someone's theological flaws
what if we just backed off?
and instead, had empathy?
imagining their experience rather than thinking
they're the enemy
or trying to give therapy
or exude some intellectual dexterity
what if we just sat presently?
being there in community

Same God

breathe
bring down the intensity
suspend your assumptions
and see the other person
as someone who was made in the image of God
the same God that we all come from

What's Up with Pet Owners?

I've never owned a pet. Or is it had a pet?
I'm not sure on the correct animal terminology,
but regardless of the proper syntax I've never had a pet.
Never had a dog.
Or a cat.
Or even a goldfish.
So there's a lot I don't understand about pet owners.

Like why do they cry so much in *Marley and Me*?
Why do they buy clothes for their dogs when they already
have a full coat of fur?
Why do they take them to the dog park so they'll socialize?
Or why do they use those in-home cameras
to just watch their dogs while they're at work?
(I don't even do that with my own kids.)

But again, I've never owned a pet.

I've never opened the door
to be greeted
by man's best friend.

Or had a cat purr
in my lap as we fell asleep on the couch
while watching late night TV.
I've never had a dog just know that I was sad.
And sit there for hours so that I wouldn't be alone.
In fact, the only time I've even been in a pet store was
when I bought a leash for my friend's pet hamster as a gag
gift for her birthday. She laughed until she cried. And then
she put that leash on her hamster with so much pride.

I still don't fully understand why. But that's pet owners for you.

You see, sometimes we encounter people like pet owners, who have lived an experience that we don't understand. And we won't. At least not until we actually take that identity-changing step of becoming a pet owner ourselves.

We can make *Marley and Me* our favorite movie.
Or people watch at the dog park.
Get a job at a pet store.
Or put a black square on Instagram.

But until we take a step of commitment
and bring a pet into our home.
And go to the dog park to socialize with other dog owners.
Buy her gifts for Christmas because she's part
of the family.
And everyone deserves a happy Christmas.

Then we will never understand the life of a pet owner.
Their experience will always be something else.
Something that we dismiss.
Something that we think is different.

But maybe we're the ones missing out.

Time

we are in a race against time
where the ticking tocks of the clock are always looming
close behind
life is short and time is swift
and by the time that we realize that time is a gift
we have missed out on time's preciousness

so focused on being in the right place at the right time
that we barely have time to breathe
trying so hard to make it to the "big time"
that we miss out on all of the times in between

for time is money
and no amount of it can buy time back
but it's only a matter of time
until your time runs flat
our greatest resource is our time
but we spend all of our time trying to collect resources
so by the time that we have finally accumulated enough
we are too old to actually enjoy them

why is it that when someone asks for the time
we will answer them in haste?
but someone asks for a moment of our time
and we say we have no time to waste?

we save time
we invest time
we take time off
but all the while time
keeps ticking away on the clock

until the sands of time have passed the line
and our time is up

so don't forget that time is precious
and it can be gone in an instant
and if you don't look up from all these distractions
then you just might miss it
for there isn't enough time for you to be
straddling the fences
you will be known for your actions
and not your intentions
don't be complacent
procrastination is the thief of time
because the one thing that time doesn't do
is time doesn't rewind

Green Pastures

i'm always so quick to move forward
addicted to the high of what's next
hoping that the next new thing will hold what i long for
but i haven't found what i'm looking for yet

i heard that contentment is found in perspective
but i always get wrapped up in what if's
i fall in love with what could be
before my eyes have adjusted to what is

i have an obsession with shortcuts
and it has haunted me with a life
that I have no lasting memory of
afraid of being stagnant
i've never grown roots deep enough
to see what my seed actually becomes

i know the Lord is my shepherd
and will make me lie down in green pastures
but i've quieted the shepherd's voice
and the empty promises of the world
are now all my hands hold

this relentless journey for a better life
has only produced more longing in my soul
my ambition confuses green pastures as red carpets
and bright lights
are the north star that my heart is drawn to

i traded depth for height
thinking the stars held the answers to my questions
but climbing the ladder of success
doesn't bring us any closer to heaven

peace can only be found in the one
who gives creation its breath
it is only when i stop trying to make my own way
that i will fully find rest

the shepherd knows my yesterdays
and my tomorrows
what i see as green pastures
God sees as hollow
what i see as dead ends
God sees what follows

The Search for "It"

i must admit
that in my never ending search for "it"
i began to drift
into a life of selfishness
my direction and my aim
was full of good intent
but i began to settle
in the end i was too content

i became a broken image
that i misprinted
my social privilege
had drifted
into my identity as a Christian

but Jesus didn't die for us to be comfortable
he didn't die for us to be content
Jesus didn't die for us to be successful
he bled and died so we could be with him
set free from desiring the approval of fallen creations

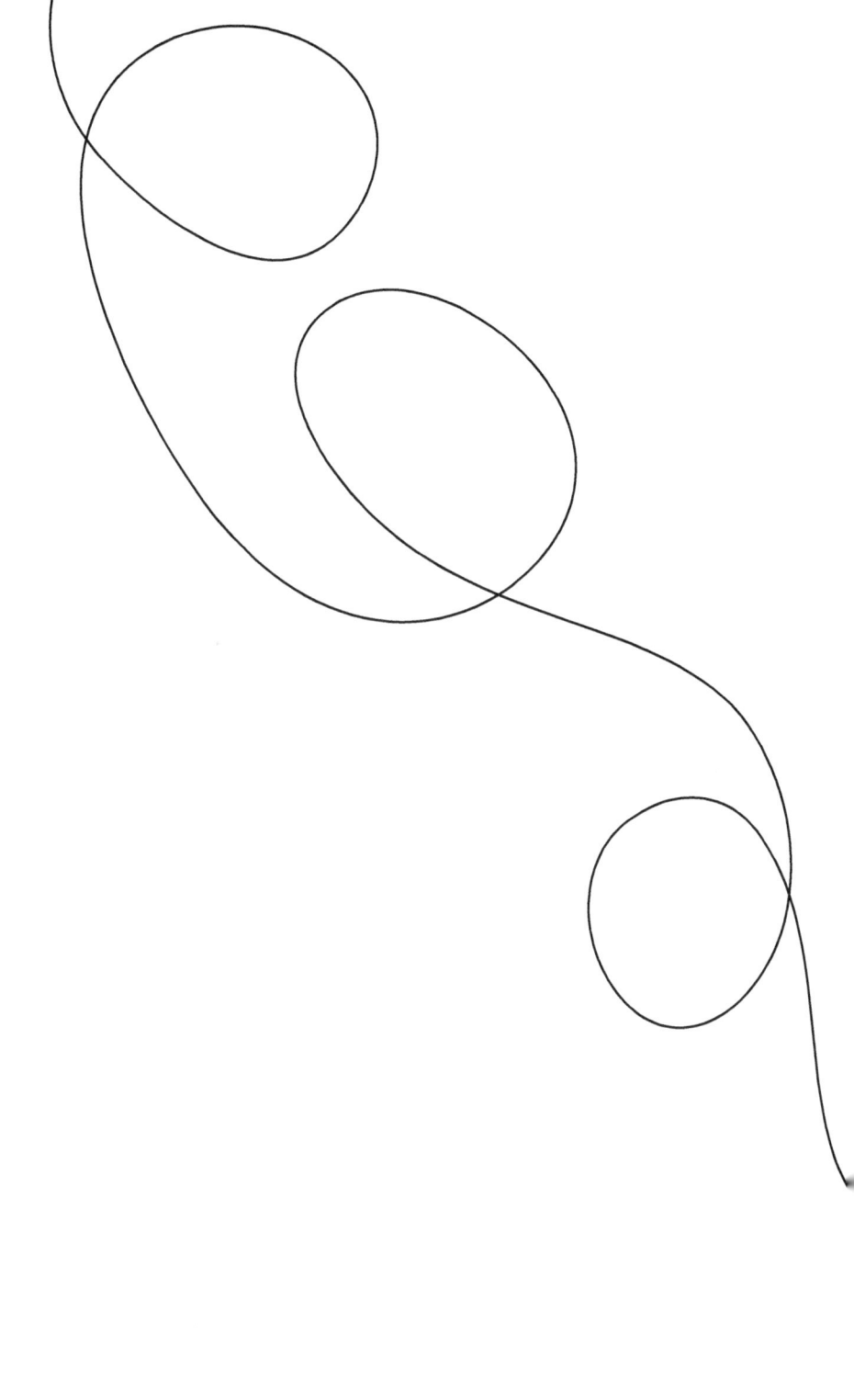

Play-Doh Jesus

Instead of being made in God's image,
we make Jesus in ours
We treat him like Play-Doh and mold him
to the desires of our hearts
We pick and choose things that he said
and chop them up into bite-size parts
We will do scriptural gymnastics
so that following him won't be so hard

So we give him ears that never hear
the negative things that we say
And eyes that are quick to see the good deeds
that we did that day
With skin that's white as snow
because Jesus would be an American!
Middle-class with conservative views
knowing that good manners in public is imperative
He'd have feet that cross the street
when scary looking people walk his way
And hands that ring themselves
over the lack of him in schools today
Shoulders that shrug off injustices
because they don't affect his day to day
A nose that he holds high
because he's been saved since second grade
Fingers that point out problems,
but are never directed back his way
Knees that never kneel
because standing tall is what makes you brave
A voice he never uses
because deeds speak louder than words

We shape Jesus into what we want him to be
rather than taking the time to learn

That he has ears that hear
the deepest thoughts of our hearts
And eyes that see all of our deeds,
the ones in the light and in the dark
With skin that's not like mine,
at my church he would stand apart
He had feet that never stopped
because he'd seek the outcast and leave the flock
His hands had holes,
but they could hold all the sins that we unfold
He had shoulders that carried a cross
because he paid a price that we would not
His nose was held low
because he humbled himself as an example to follow
His fingers pointed at religious leaders
highlighting their self-seeking motives and intentions
His knees stayed kneeling
as a sign of humble submission
He used his voice for those who felt unheard
But when he was confronted with arrogance
he was never afraid to speak harsh words

You see when we take out the context
or add our own context that wasn't really there
We create a version of Jesus
that says if you're not like me
Then I don't care

Complacency

my throat is an open grave
my tongue has mastered deceit
my heart is wrapped in chains
to where I can't even hear it beat
my pride couldn't take the taste of defeat
as I got lost on the path while playing hide-and-seek

so much motion
no movement
like a hamster in a wheel
where my Bible lays idle
and mind just reels
stacking idols on idols
that I can see touch and feel
getting lazy in my walk
but I'm too prideful to kneel

lift my head high and brush my shoulders off
but I feel like I'm brushing boulders off
because I'm getting too soft in my convictions
pushing the boundary by inches
as I'm straddling the fences
complacency has inched in
and become my daily addiction

Doing vs Being

We are so busy doing instead of being
Trying so hard to "do right"
That we often miss the meaning behind our "good deeds"

We haven't been saved by anything that we have done
So why do we focus on our good deeds
instead of the blood of the Son?
Why do we have perfect attendance at church
but during the week don't read one single scripture?
And when we are faced with a problem
we go to family and friends before God for the answer?

It's because we have the relationship backwards.

It's like we are walking around with an empty frame,
but we are missing the actual picture.
We have the outside covered, but we are missing
the actual fixture.

God's love is a promise, not based on performance
It's based purely on the fact that He adores us.
It's not a promise with stipulations and hidden agendas
There is no fine print hidden beneath the Scriptures.

So start being in reliance on God
And stop doing things to earn God's love
Plant yourself by the stream of God's beauty
Allow the Spirit to continue the process of pruning
For the more you abide
then the more good fruit will start producing
Because being in the presence of the King
Is better than doing anything.

Clean as Dirt

when we enter this earth
we're as clean as dirt
no matter our works
we've been dead since birth
i know that may hurt
but it's Adam's curse
when he ate the fruit
perfection dispersed
and now we're immersed in Satan's purse
we come out of the womb riding in a hearse
thank God that Christ came to reimburse our worth

Good Intentions

I was born of good intentions
but good intentions don't bring salvation
they just build you up on a slippery foundation
due to lack of information
we've believed the lie that being good enough
will get you through the pearly gates
but no matter how good we are
our efforts are a waste
for without the atoning sacrifice of Jesus
then we are just running in place
we could love like Mother Theresa
but without Christ we've lost the race

Fully Connected | Immensely Lonely

we live in a world where technology
connects us further than anytime in human history
yet isolation and loneliness
is so much greater than it used to be
and honestly it's not some mystical mystery
we make connections without establishing roots
living in the world of social media
but being social is the furthest thing from the truth
where the winds of the culture
blow us away before we bear any relational fruit
literally starving ourselves on our constant pursuit
of what's trending
of what's trendy
we're pretending
over extending

no one is real

we just cover up our problems
suppressing what we feel
we've traded being truly known by others
for cultural appeal
and so we're left with an emptiness
that no instagram filter can heal
a generation held prisoner to their camera reel

Confessions of a Technology Addict

confession #1:
the first thing i do whenever i wake up in the morning
is look at my phone
before kissing my wife good morning
i scroll through twitter to see what stories
are being overblown
i check my emails even though i won't be at work
for another two hours
it's like i have this invisible cord
and my phone is what gives me power

confession #2:
i text and drive
(sorry mom)
convincing myself that i have mastered
how to hold my phone at three and my wheel at nine
so no one can notice that i'm only halfway aware
of their presence when they drive by
for some reason i think my immediate response
is worth more than my life
and that operating a motor vehicle at a speed
faster than an ostrich can run
isn't living life on the edge enough
adrenaline junkie or overstimulated addict,
both too unaware of how precious life is

confession #3:
i spend my nights
binge watching netflix

while playing games on my phone

as if this walking dead episode
isn't engaging enough on its own
i need two screens, i need two things
because my mind likes to roam

but instead of teaching it discipline,
i just let it go
constantly restless
i'm searching for a new way to scratch the itch
but it's getting more and more impossible to resist

confession #4:

i care   (a lot)
about how many likes my instagram post has
the amount of self-affirmation that those red hearts
can provide is the definition of pitiful
i first realized things had crossed a line
whenever i first said happy birthday to my dad
through a caption on instagram
rather than actually calling him
(sorry dad)

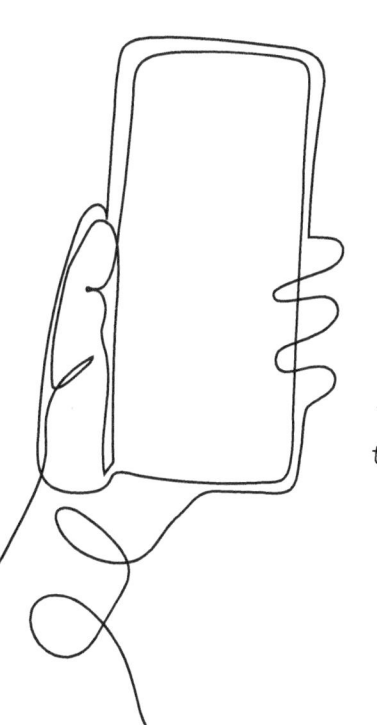

confession #5:
i have maybe three friends
that if i didn't upload
life updates on instagram
they'd actually know
what's going on in my life
and i'm not sure i have
a single friend who actually knows
how non-instagram me is doing
but idk if i even know how i'm doing
i never look up from my phone
long enough to process
the world around me

Loneliness of Social Media

i look at my phone where i have hundreds of contacts
yet at the same time i have no one to contact
so i scroll on instagram
for a way to have the time pass
as the world moves around me
i'm like a sun in a time lapse

the world keeps spinning
yet i never move
snap chat after snap chat
but i'm just alone in my room
looking at all the dope things
my friends get to do
becoming more and more lonely
the more that I scroll through

Copycat Creations

when was the last time
that you created something?
when was the last time
that you looked into an empty medium
and you put your soul into it?

i bet that it's been awhile
(and that's a shame)
because you have a voice
and a story to be named
a creation
with an identity to be claimed

but we live our lives
listening to the ideas of other people
content letting the content
that we consume
be the place that we get our views

Does Anyone Know That You're a Christian?

does anyone know that you're a Christian?
because if they don't then they need to
there are people who need you
people in your life whom the Holy Spirit
is calling you to speak to
because evangelism isn't just meant
for people standing behind the pulpit.
it's meant for every Christian
in every instance
so don't keep your faith hidden
Christ already has risen
and his life has already been given
people just need someone to tell them
they need to show them
they need someone to love them
they need you

Secret Faith

is your faith something that you keep secret?
thinking that others don't need it
so you keep it in your pocket
and then on sundays you pull it out to feed it?
standing there in worship
singing "thank you Jesus"
but once service ends you slip him back into your pocket
swallow that praise and lock it
suppressing His true knowledge
making Him your second option

it goes back to Adam and Eve in the garden
suppressing His truth for ours
until we see that our faces
are on the back of a milk carton
because our true self
the self shaped in the image of God
has long been gone
and replaced with an idolatrous image
that is so far off

As One

We are called to be One
One Body
One Spirit
Saved by God's Son
Who for our salvation descended from above
Who while being fully divine
Jesus embraced our humanity in His love

Who without vanity, and complete humility
Sacrificed His life so that we would have life
Christ emptied himself
Taking on the form of a servant
And even though he didn't deserve it
He was obedient to the point of death
Now that act of service is as humble as it gets

And yet we, Christ's Church
who are created as One
Are a complete mess

To the outside, we are known more for conflict and divisions
Than for carrying out God's divine vision
We are seen more often upholding political party directives
Than upholding where Scripture directs us
We prepare more for arguments and debates
Than preparing to be vessels of God's grace

So focused on winning that we've lost sight
of why we are running the race

So what if we memorized a few scriptures?
What's the point if we don't live out
what that text actually means?
What's the purpose of knowing
the original Greek form of Love?
If hate still controls our tongue when we speak?

We all deserve the same death
We all are as filthy as it gets
Jesus came to pay off the same debt
So we aren't any better than the rest

We are called to be One
One Body
One Spirit
Saved by God's Son
Who for our salvation descended from above
Who while being fully divine
Embraced our humanity in His love

Before the Red Sea

We think that for us to be truly living in God's calling
then the Red Sea has to part.
Whenever truly Moses spent forty years as a shepherd
before that burning bush ever sparked.
For four decades Moses had no following, yet he remained.
He literally threw away a life of fame
to stand up for injustice
Knowing the consequence would be a life
of watching sheep graze.

But he knew that his identity and calling
wasn't valued on the perception of others.
And it is that humility that kept him grounded
so whenever he did experience God's miracles and wonders
He never thought he was better than his brothers.

Except Me / Accept Me

We spend our days on earth wondering "who will accept me?"
While God is in heaven saying "hey, just accept me."
"You want everyone else's approval...except me."

Content with the Fine Print

I'm going to live my life not afraid of the background
Content with the fine print
I don't need to stand out
God moves and I follow
Open hands
No bravado
In the limelight or the shadows
He's in charge of all my tomorrows

Bruised Cheeks

How did you turn the cheek
when they **twisted** the words you said?
How did you have your Last Supper
with a man who wanted you **dead**?
How did you not expose their pride-filled lies
but continued **letting** them spread?
Knowing that rather than a Savior
they'd make you a **scapegoat** instead.

Judas **betrayed** you
for silver
Peter denied you
denied you 3 times
The Jews chose Barabbas
Yet you were nothing but kind.

Why?

You didn't defend your honor
Or **fight back**
Or justify your actions
You turned the other cheek
Silently surrendered
And got **killed** for their infractions.

Killed for **my** infractions.

But since you lifted no defense
For my offense
My cheeks will represent
Your sacrificial gift
I will loosen my grip
On my need to defend with my lips
I will follow your script
I will choose to forgive

In hopes that the repeated
turning of my cheek
will spread seeds

And from these seeds roots will grow deep

And one day branches will grow fruit from that tree
And that fruit will feed multitudes
from the bruises of my cheeks.
That is my hope
That others would feast
From the fruit of my bruised cheeks
Fruit that my eyes might never see
Eyes that never saw your face
A face bruised from my mistakes.

Death by Suicide

The other day I thought I heard your voice
I didn't know my heart could beat that fast
I turned around expecting to see your goofy smile
But then I remembered that I'll never see you again

I still remember every word from that phone call
And the knot in my stomach as I heard Death by Suicide

How could I not have seen what must've been so obvious?
How could I be your friend and not notice?
Was I so absorbed with my constant chaos
That I overlooked the tornado that you lived in?
Or did you just keep me at a distance?
And what I viewed as friendship
You just viewed as an acquaintance

Trick or Treat

Depression is like living as if every day is Halloween
But instead of wearing a monster mask on the outside
You mask the monster that's inside
handing out fake smiles to family and friends
like passing out candy to every person
that knocks on your door

Afraid that if you tell somebody
about the monster inside it'll destroy them
So by wearing your mask
the only person the monster can hurt is you
You smile through white knuckles
You'll smile to the end
Thinking they'll never understand
if you try to let them in
The greatest trick is living with depression
while nobody knows
And their treat is never knowing
how dark those thoughts can go

End the Stigma

In 8th grade my best friend broke his foot
and I couldn't wait to sign my name on his cast
I wonder if someone will ever ask me
to sign their bottle of Prozac

Probably not

Because so many people see mental illness
as mental weakness
As excuses, not sickness
That these conversations are needless
They just need to spend more time with Jesus

But depression is not a sin
It does not mean you're spiritually weak
It does not mean your faith is incomplete

We need to end the stigma and stop giving shallow answers
You don't tell someone to pray more or worship harder
if they want to defeat cancer
So stop giving mental illness a different standard

Our fear of sitting in uncomfortable spaces
is sending people to an early grave
There are people battling mental demons
that would give Goliath nightmares
And if we don't equip them with the proper tools
Then they'll be ripped to shreds
while reciting hollow prayers

We need to end the stigma
And tell people they are not alone
1.4 million people around the world
died by suicide last year
and that number will only continue to grow
Unless we remove the mask of our own

Simple Days

I wish we could go back to the days
to when picking your nose in public was okay
AKA the simple days
The days when popularity in school
was judged by your lunch box
(Power Rangers and Ninja Turtles always held the top spots)
Just listening to Kidz Bop while popping Pop Rocks
Sleepovers with friends always felt like time stopped

We would spend the whole day playing Game Boys
(Pokémon Red Version was our main choice)
We tried to skateboard
Thinking that we were Tony Hawk
We could hardly pop an ollie but we felt we were on top

We'd then go out to Cici's for the pizza buffet
Pockets packed with quarters for the arcade
We'd buy those sticky hands that stick on the wall
And maybe a couple of those glow-in-the-dark bouncy balls
We'd mix every soda and call that a suicide
(That was before depression took the life
of some friends of mine)
Now that word holds a different memory in my mind
But when I think of them I just go back to those times

When our biggest worry in life
was how to multiply and divide
And whenever we would cry Mom was there to dry our eye
When our heroes in life were people who could fly
And we had no concept of what it meant to die

Repentance I

Dear Aaron,

Remember growing up in Sunday School
when we learned the nursery rhyme:
"He's got the whole world in His hands.
He's got the whole world in His hands."

And then we got older and you were diagnosed
with an anxiety disorder?
As your church family, we didn't understand
the desert of distress that you walked in daily
Our efforts of support were telling you to pray more
So you prayed more than I had in my entire life
But when your anxieties didn't subside
We questioned your heart
instead of the chemical imbalance inside
I'm sorry our understanding of God never grew past
Our Sunday School nursery rhymes

To us, your anxiety was proof
that you didn't trust God's plans
That you didn't believe that the whole world
was in God's hands
We saw your anxiety as something that could be prayed away
And in the process we caused you to pull away
Our craving for quick fixes and easy answers
Made us look like the blind leading the blind
Rather than being vessels for the power
that makes blind men see

So when you stopped showing up at church
we thought you accepted defeat
But you just accepted what we told you to believe
That your anxiety made you weak
That your anxiety made your faith incomplete

I'm so sorry.

P.S.
You can be a Christian and be on Xanax.
You can be a Christian and go to therapy.
Actually, it's preferred

Repentance II

Dear Trey,

Remember growing up in Sunday School
when we learned the nursery rhyme:
"Jesus loves the little children, all the children
of the world. Red and yellow, black and white.
They are precious in his sight."

But that wasn't your church experience….
you always felt like an outsider
And that community that you desired
That community that we preached about and broadcasted
And said "just get involved and it'll change your life"

You realized only worked if you were white

Because you went and you tried
But every time you would lift up a prayer
for injustice or police hate crimes
We would look at you with confusion in our eyes
Never knowing why week after week
you would pray for something so political

I found it odd when you said
you felt the loneliest at church
I mean everyone loved you
People went to church because of you
Then you asked why you were the only one
to bring up racism over the years
How our silence on the topic made it clear
That we lived in two different spheres
That people might hear you with their ears
But they would never feel your fears
Or the pain within your tears
Because if the church saw your skin color
as precious as it is in God's sight
Then you wouldn't have to be the only one
standing up to fight

I'm sorry that I left you alone to fight battles
that you never asked for

Repentance III

Dear Hannah,

Remember growing up in Sunday School
when we learned the nursery rhyme:
"Here is the church, here is the steeple,
open the doors and see all the people."

I'm sorry that when you opened those doors to our church
Those people inside spoke as loud gongs and clanging symbols
Instead of the loving grace that God resembles

We were wolves in sheeps' disguise
Our love was wrapped in lies
The sacred home for Christ's bride
Had been infiltrated by elitism and pride

We were a church of cliques
And you quickly got eclipsed
Hidden in the shadows
Being overlooked and missed
Not feeling any more welcome
than before you walked in
Not realizing that church was like
reliving high school all over again

I'm ashamed that I didn't greet you
I was more focused on the people I knew
Than those I didn't
The Church should be a harbor for every Christian
But we left you out in the storms of life
Until the waves swallowed you whole

We say we want to save souls
But our goal was really just to save the ones
that fit our mold

I'm sorry I was so focused on shaking hands
with my best friend
That I wasn't the hands and feet of Jesus
to the new girl who walked in

You deserved better